Searching for the Ox

Other books by Louis Simpson

Poetry

      The Arrivistes: Poems 1940-1949
      Good News of Death and Other Poems
      A Dream of Governors
      At the End of the Open Road
      Selected Poems
      Adventures of the Letter I

Prose

      James Hogg: A Critical Study
      Riverside Drive
      An Introduction to Poetry
      North of Jamaica
      Three on the Tower: The Lives and Works of Ezra
        Pound, T. S. Eliot and William Carlos Williams

Searching for the Ox

Louis Simpson

Phyllis Hoge

William Morrow and Company, Inc.
New York   1976

Copyright © 1971, 1973, 1974, 1975, 1976 by Louis Simpson

Poems in this collection were first published in magazines,
newspapers and anthologies. The author gratefully acknowledges
permission from the editors of these publications to reprint the poems
here.

*The Listener, The Paris Review, The American Poetry Review, The
Times Literary Supplement, The Columbia Forum, The Southern
Review, New Statesman, The Ohio Review, Critical Quarterly, The
Hampden-Sydney Poetry Review, Decal Poetry Review, Present
Tense, London Magazine, Ten Good Poems, Dacotah Territory,
Sumac, Newsday, Workshop New Poetry, Forum, The Beloit Poetry
Journal, The Falcon, Chicago Review.*
"Searching for the Ox" and "The Shelling Machine" originally
appeared in *The New Yorker.*

Printed in the United States of America.

2   3   4   5   80   79   78   77   76

Library of Congress Cataloging in Publication Data

Simpson, Louis Aston Marantz (date)
    Searching for the ox.

    I.   Title
PS3537.I75S4   811'.5'4   75-40950
ISBN 0-688-03008-4

Book design: H. Roberts

For Saul Galin, critic and friend

Contents

IV *Further Adventures of the Letter I*

Preface

Most of the time I lived at school. There was plenty to say and do—a hundred and thirty young males penned within walls on the top of a mountain.

But during vacations, especially the long summers, days would go by when I hardly spoke to anyone. I had an older brother. Our parents were divorced. Our mother had gone back to America and we lived with our father and stepmother. After a while no one was invited to the house. Our father was a lawyer; he was accustomed to dealing with cases; I suppose that he did not want his own life examined in the same way. So we were isolated. I spent most of the days by myself, communing with sea, sky, and my thoughts. The opening poem in this book, "Venus in the Tropics," tells of this period.

We lived on Kingston harbor. Stretches of the shore were unfenced and apparently belonged to no one. You could walk along the beach without encountering another human soul. There were sea birds and beasts; many of them would be washed up on shore sooner or later. It wasn't unusual, on looking up, to see a line of porpoises or the fin of a shark cutting the surface.

I still have dreams in which I am walking on a beach of white sand. There was such a place. To reach it you had to drive out of Kingston on a road that passed through a tunnel. Beyond lay a beach where waves of the outer sea came rolling in. The sand was fine and there were shells of all shapes and colors. There were pieces of flint, and yellow seeds as hard and smooth as stones, and flat brown seeds called "horse eyes." In the dream I am picking them up as fast as I can, for I shall soon have to leave.

Isolation turned me to reading stories and poems. It was stories I was after in either case; I didn't want fine emotions as much as I wanted something to happen to break the silence of the island. I read Conrad's "Youth" and *Typhoon* against a backdrop of palm trees and waves as exotic as any in his tales. But there was a difference: in Conrad there was passion and adventure. I saw none in the life around me.

Therefore I set about creating adventures of my own and setting them down on paper. This may be why I believe that we make our lives by ourselves, their meaning and excitement. It is generally thought that writers have a point of view and write in order to put it across. I am inclined to think the opposite: they write and so create a point of view.

When I first read Camus I was struck by the similarity between his early years in Algeria and mine in Jamaica. In the tropics where nature is everything and man is nothing, a man may decide that he alone is responsible for his life. When I left Jamaica and went to New York I felt a difference between my sense of the world and that held by friends who had grown up in the towns of New York and New Jersey. They thought in social terms and were aiming to get ahead in the world. Later, when I was in the army and they were in medical school or one of the other professions, I felt the distance increased immeasurably.

*

Searching for the Ox is in four parts. The first two parts describe the life of a young man coming from a background similar to my own. Poems in the third part are more meditative; they are about a way of life. And the concluding section is made up of poems rising out of my interests as a writer.

Many of the poems are narrative or contain elements of narrative, for I wish to represent life even when there is an idea to be expressed. The idea should be felt, seeming to rise out of an event rather than being imposed.

But though these poems have their origin in things I have seen or heard, they are not, as Gatsby says, "just personal." Poetry has frequently been based on personal experience, but the incident that moves us has been transformed in the telling from the merely personal into a work of art. The poet dares to imagine and to explore the unknown.

Beside the narrative element in these poems, I am struck by how much they attempt to capture the atmosphere of a time, the concrete specificity of a place. I might have put Conrad's words in front of this book: "My task which I am trying to achieve is, by the power of the written word to make you hear, to make you feel—it is, before all, to make you see."

I have moved from place to place. After the war I lived for a while in France—the poem titled "Lorenzo" speaks of this. I worked in a publishing house in Manhattan. In years that followed I lived in Italy, in California, and England. Now from my window I gaze out on the north shore of Long Island.

Walking along the shore I am aware that nothing much has changed. The tide comes in here, across mud flats covered with weeds. The sides of the channel are carpeted with stalks of dead weeds, thick and springy underfoot. There are some boards nailed together, half buried in sand; I sit on them and contemplate the backs of houses on the far side of the channel. A few feet away there's an upheaval in the sand, an inch-high eruption. A living creature slides up and halfway out. A saffron-colored packet. It's the flash of its withdrawal, however, that really makes you know it's alive. 13

Then I notice there are holes in the sand all around.
A dozen tunnels with alternative exits. Down there
it must be like the photographs you used to see of the
Maginot Line underground: long tunnels with pale
Frenchmen playing cards, looking up at the photographer.
"Drôle de guerre!"

Sea and shore are the same. If I followed them
around I would come to the shore where I used to
walk as a boy. But I have changed; I am different from the
boy and the man I used to be, the one I call Peter.

These changes cry out for a life that does not change.
The less we are at home in the world, the more
we bear witness to that other life.

I
Venus in the Tropics

Venus in the Tropics

1

One morning when I went over to Bournemouth
it was crowded with American sailors—
chubby faces like Jack Oakie
chewing gum and cracking wise.

Pushing each other into the pool,
bellyflopping from the diving boards,
piling on the raft to sink it,
hanging from the rings, then letting go.

Later, when I went into Kingston
to exchange some library books,
they were everywhere, buying souvenirs,
calabash gourds and necklaces made of seeds.

On Saturday night at the Gaiety
they kept talking and making a noise.
When the management asked them to stop
they told it to get wise, to fly a kite, to scram.

2

We drove down to Harbor Street
with Mims ("She isn't your mother.
You ought to call her by some affectionate nickname—
why don't you call her Mims?")

There were two American cruisers,

the turrets and guns distinctly visible,
and some destroyers—I counted four.

The crews were coming ashore in launches.
As each group walked off the dock
we noticed a number of women
wearing high heels. They went up to the sailors
and engaged them in conversation.

"You've seen enough," said Mims.
"In fact, you may have seen too much."
She started the Buick, shifting into gear
swiftly with a gloved hand.

She always wore gloves and a broad hat.
To protect her complexion,
she told us. She was extremely sensitive.
All redheaded people were.

"She's a redhead, like Clara Bow,"
our father wrote in his letter.

"The Red Death," said my grandmother
twenty years later, on Eastern Parkway
in Brooklyn. We were talking about my father.
She thought he must have been ill—
not in his right mind—to marry a typist
and leave her practically everything.

How else to explain it, such an intelligent man?

3

The American warships left.
Then the *Empress of Britain*

came and stayed for a few days
during which the town was full of tourists.
Then, once more, the harbor was empty.

I sat by the pool at Bournemouth
reading *Typhoon*.
I had the pool all to myself,
the raft, the diving boards, and the rings.
There wasn't a living soul.

Not a voice—just rustling palm leaves
and the tops of the coconuts
moving around in circles.

In the afternoon a wind sprang up,
blowing from the sea to land,
covering the harbor with whitecaps.

It smelled of shells and seaweed,
and something else—perfume.

Dinner at the Sea-View Inn

1

Peter said, "I'd like some air."

"That's a good idea," said Marie's father.
"Why don't you young people go for a walk?"

Marie glanced at her mother.
Something passed between them. A warning.

2

When Peter and Marie walked through the dining room
everyone stared.

I just think so,
he reminded himself, and said,
"Fitzgerald says that nobody thinks about us
as much as we think they do."

"Who's he?" said Marie. "Another of your favorite
      authors?"

3

She wanted to know where he was taking her.

"I just had to get out of there.
Wouldn't it be great to hire a taxi
and just keep going?"

"Why?" said Marie.

"It's a wonderful night."

"I'd rather have my own car," said Marie.

4

"I'm getting cold," said Marie.
"How much further are we going?"

"All right," he said.
                    And they walked back.

"When I was a child," said Peter,
"I used to think that the waves were cavalry . . .
the way they come in, curling over."

She said, "Is that what you were in,
the calvary?"

He laughed. "Calvary? For Christ's sake . . ."

5

"Did you have a good walk?" said Marie's father.

Marie said something to her mother.

Shortly after, Mr. Shulman ordered the car,

and they all drove back to New York.

They let Peter out in front of his building
on West Eighty-fourth Street, saying goodnight.
All but Marie . . . She still sat stiffly,
unsmiling. She had been offended.

6

Everything was just as he'd left it . . .
the convertible couch,
the reading lamp and chair,
and the stand with the typewriter.

He undressed and went to bed,
and turned out the light.

Lying in bed, hands clasped beneath his head,
listening . . .

to the stopping and starting of traffic
in the street five floors below.
And the opening of the elevator,
and the sound of feet going down the corridor.

The Psyche of Riverside Drive

1

The wind was packed with cold.
He pushed against it, over to the Drive
and down a block—watching his step
so as not to slip in the icy slush.

He went through the ritual of entering a building—
speaking on the intercom, the buzzing
and opening of the second door.
He trod the path worn in the carpet
from the entrance to the elevator.

On the right the girl in marble,
Psyche, was in her niche,
her breasts as round, her arms as smooth as ever.
One hand went to her heart; the other
lifted a lamp. It shed no light,
for the globe and the bulb were smashed.
The couch in the opposite wall
where Eros used to lie was empty.

He rang for the elevator.
It came, and he ascended—
smelling some cooking soup or stew,
like the smells that waft through a ship.

And when he walked down the corridor
it seemed that he could feel the engines.
These were cabins, dimly lit.
But all the voyage would be inward.

The people who lived here feared for their lives.

Many had moved to Connecticut.
Those who remained, when you rang,
peered at you through a peephole.
Then the eye withdrew and you heard the bolt
     drawn back.

2

It was no grumbling dwarf
or troll who stood in the door,
but Nil Admirari, the Professor.

"Peter," he said, "well well,
I'm glad to see you."

He said, sometimes he thought of Peter
and wondered what he was doing.
Journalism? Well, he smiled,
experience was a hard school . . .
Peter silently finished the sentence:
"but fools will learn in no other."

What would he have? Mrs. Wilson—
for so the Professor referred to his wife—
was, he dared say, making tea.
Or would Peter like something stronger?

He would? Good, so would he.
And he disappeared to find whiskey.
Leaving Peter in excellent company . . .
all *The Great Books*, with the *Syntopicon*,

and the novels of Henry James.
For at that time, after the war,
everybody was either reading Melville
or else they were reading James.

24

In the words of another famous novelist,
there had been nothing like it
since the craze for table-turning.

3

Professor Wilson was telling his former student
that the visible world was a dream.

The student thought the Professor was the dream.
How could I, he wondered, ever have listened to this?
He said, "If the world is a dream,
then what shall we say dreams are?
We'll have to think up a new set of words.
For there is a difference between dreaming and waking.
Even if we say that life is a dream
that only feels as though it were real,
the feeling is there. We have to deal with it.
I think," he concluded, "we are playing with words."

"That's it," said the Professor,
"that's just the point."
Then he said, in the special voice
like an Englishman's he used for poetry:
"I have seen violence, I have seen violence.
Give thy heart after letters."

Mrs. Wilson came in.
She looked anemic and had gray hair.

"Margaret," said the Professor,
"you remember Peter.
We are having an interesting discussion."

Mrs. Wilson smiled wanly.
She had seen so many promising students,

and listened to so many interesting discussions.

4

He walked over to Broadway,
and kept on walking, though it was cold,
passing the entrance to the subway.
He wanted physical exertion—the solidity
and resonance of the sidewalk under his feet.

The avenue extended—buildings
with windows, rows of blinds and curtains.

He passed the Far East Restaurant,
a laundromat, a liquor store.
A cigar store . . .

Then the Calderon. They were playing
Amor y Calor, with Francisca Gonzales.

He looked at the face in the mantilla.
There is always some passionate race
that has just arrived in America.

And a fragrance, *pimienta*,
the wind brings over the sea.

Lorenzo

I

In the mornings I would write, sitting on the
      veranda.
In the afternoons I would go to the village
and then for a swim or a walk.

I was meditating on the embankment
of an abandoned railroad
when a man came by, one of the villagers,
a clerk in string-tie and coat.
He struck up a conversation.
When I told him that I wrote,
he said there was an English novelist
named Ascham living in the vicinity.

I had heard of Harry Ascham.
I went to the bookshop and bought one of his works.
This in hand, I approached the villa
where he lived, according to the Frenchman.

II

Upon my entering
he seized the decanter of whiskey
on the table before him and fled
upstairs, and his wife came down.

I explained—I only wanted to talk—
and she went upstairs. I heard some grumbling,
then he reappeared. In a while,
with drinking whiskey and reminiscing
he warmed. He spoke of Ez

and Tom Eliot
and D. H. Lawrence (Lorenzo).

He spoke of Hilary Thorpe
the poet. Whereupon I put my foot in it,
saying, "Is she still alive?" ,
not knowing they had once been married.
Ascham looked startled and reached for the decanter
that Sybil, his present wife, kept filled.

He spoke of *The Egoist* and *The Criterion*,
and more about Lawrence . . .
with his TB, the onlie Begetter.
"Did you know," he said, "he lived here, on an
        island?"

III

I hired a fisherman's boat,
furrowing the sea, and came
to Lawrence's island.

The path was littered with equipment,
moldy black leather and messkits
left by the retreating *Wehrmacht*.
On the day of the invasion . . .
thunder . . . the horizon rippling.

The naval guns had fastened on Lawrence's villa
and blown it to bits.
There were only parts of walls
and windows framing the sky.

Little did he care,

being gone to Australia
and America . . . back to Italy
and, finally, to the shades.

Sitting among these stones
I listened to the dry leaves rustling
and thought of a poet's life.
Genus irritabile vatum.
Because he longs for Beauty
with man he grows enraged.
Driven here and there . . . If he does find
    a home,
the world comes along and smashes it.
Just as frequently, he smashes it himself.

Most people can hardly understand it,
content as they are to stay in one place.
Like the cicada, to make one sound repeatedly
all their lives. Monotonous. Like the rasp
of the spring of a watch being wound.

      IV

Ascham said, "Lawrence was a genius
but . . ."
           Frieda wore long drawers.

When they were living in Taos,
Lawrence dug with his own two hands
a ditch a mile long to bring water.
In the middle of the desert
he made an English garden . . . flowers

such as you still see in Nottingham
outside a miner's cottage.

You could see the drawers hanging on the line
on washdays. Lawrence was a Puritan.
Only an English Puritan
would have written *Lady Chatterley's Lover*.

He wouldn't have been such a fool.

V

I was leaving for Paris
and called to say goodbye.

Ascham had been drinking heavily.
He spoke of his life in California—
writing scripts, he said, for illiterates.
They couldn't even speak their own Yiddish.

He gave me advice: "If you want to be a writer,
write! Don't wait to be asked.
Write reviews. Write articles. Write anything.
And don't think you're a genius."

At the gate looking back
I saw Ascham standing at a window
looking out. He was joined by his wife . . .
as though they were expecting someone

who comes up the path and shouts
"Where are you? Where are you hiding,

Ascham? Come out, you ridiculous man!"

He throws his pack on the table
and puts his boots up on a chair.
He shows you the flower in his buttonhole
he's picked, and wants its name.
You ought to know—it came out of your garden.

He's come a long way
from some far world to this,
bending his neck to the yoke
of local speech and custom . . .
whatever smells of the earth.

He wants to sit up all night talking—
not just about you,
but life. What do you think?
Or has it all been reminiscing?

He wants to hear all the news.
In a few hours he'll be leaving,
resuming his interrupted journey

from the pier-end of the street
to Arcturus and the stars.

II

The Company of Flesh and Blood

I have wished to keep the reader in the company of flesh and blood.

—WORDSWORTH

The Springs at Gadara

I spent five years in publishing—
feet on the bottom desk drawer, the foetal
        position,
reading *Crossways, A Novel*
and *The Life of Elbert Hubbard.*

At day's end, depending on the weather,
I would walk—acrosstown and up,
sometimes uptown and across.
Looking in the windows exhibiting
golf, ice skates, ski equipment,
Sweetville Candy U. S. A.,
a tour of France or Italy.
At the movie marquee advertising
No Morals and Midnight Frolics Adults Only.

Autumn is best, the feeling of excitement
at twilight, the lights going on.
Beauty moves in the crowd up ahead
on the avenue. There she is again—
a flash of color vanishing
in the cool, illusory air.
Where is she going? Who lives where she lives?

Then I would be in the side streets
with Jesus signs and boarded windows.
Not because I am underpaid,
I told myself. I like these shabby streets
where everything is expected.

I would climb three flights to the apartment,
and flop. Then it was dark, with lights
going by, flashes on the ceiling.

So, without effort, time was passing.
I might have fought for Israel.
I might have been writing a novel
the size of Proust's. Two pages a day
for five years—you figure it!
There were times when I would try to write,
but soon tire, taking off my glasses
and covering my eyes. Like Swann.
This would set off a train of thought.

Finally I'd say to hell with it,
and decide to spend another evening with
        Gallagher.
He too was in publishing. We used to go
        to parties
and meet successful authors.
They didn't sit around discussing *le mot juste*—
they talked about their royalties,
and the latest rumors—what Paramount
had paid for the movie rights
to the new novel by Jones, Capote or Mailer.

Gallagher drank. One evening
when I arrived, his door was open.
He was lying on the floor, dead drunk.
He had left the phonograph on,
the turntable going around,
playing "My Funny Valentine" over and over.

When I look back at myself
it is like looking through a window

and seeing another person.
I see him trying to lift Gallagher
onto the sofa. Then giving it up.
He comes across to the window
and stands there, looking out.

Who knows, there may be another,
a third, who from where he stands
in the night can see us both.

*

One day I was leafing through a manuscript
taken at random from the slush pile.
It was titled *The Springs at Gadara.*

The epigraph explained: there once was a philosopher
named Jamblicus, who by magic raised
the spirits of Eros and Anteros
close by the springs at Gadara.

Anteros . . . I stared at the name.
Eros I knew, but Anteros . . .

Words are realities. They have the power
to make us feel and see.
I had a vision of an oasis,
and some Arabs sitting on the ground.

And myself, in the midst of it,
chained to a horizontal beam.
I was pushing it around in a circle,
and a heavy millstone rolled
in a groove as the beam went around.

All the time I had spent in publishing,
sitting at a desk . . . actually, I had
       been laboring
under a spell. Anteros.
It was time for Eros to put in an appearance.

As I thought so, the chain fell off.
I started walking away.
Nothing sprang up behind me
and no one uttered a sound.

When I had gone some distance
I looked back. There was the oasis,
the palm trees, and the Arabs
in the same positions, sitting on the ground.

I could see the horizontal beam
and some other poor devil pushing it,
making the stone go around.

The Stevenson Poster

Talking to someone your own age
who has made a million dollars
you realize that time is passing,
and one thing is sure, you'll never make
      a million.

He had just bought into a cooperative—
the penthouse, with a magnificent view.
He showed it to me from the patio.
Behind us a roar . . . the housewarming party . . .
the sound poured outward, over the Atlantic.

"Twelve rooms," he had said—
I was impressed.
Especially by one room that had nothing in it
but a tank that glowed deep blue . . .
a tropical aquarium
with coral reefs, places to go in and out.

One fish was adhering to the side of the tank—
"He does the sanitation," said my host.
When I thought of my one and a half rooms
with the Salvation Army furniture,
I could have applied for the job myself.

There were paintings by De Kooning and Hans
      Hofmann.

In the library, next to a certificate
stating that William Francis Heilbrun
had been "pledged to trout release,"

hung a poster of Adlai Stevenson—
the one where he was running for president
with a hole in the sole of his shoe.

*

Bill and Marion owned a house in East Hampton.
They asked me out one Saturday.
The children had just been given a sailboat—
there was great interest and excitement.
Marion would say, "They're too far out,"
and Bill would tell her not to worry.
Then she went back to *Harper's Bazaar*
and her nails. Whenever I think about her
she is wearing dark glasses and reading
        Harper's Bazaar
or *Vogue*, and polishing her nails.

I would have said they were happy,
but the next time I saw Bill Heilbrun
he and Marion were getting a divorce.

Like other apparently happy couples
they had felt they were "missing out on life."
They kept thinking, Is this all?
Nothing seemed to help, not even analysis,
so they decided to separate, to "start a new
        life."

They had sold the twelve-room apartment.
The day they moved, he sat down with the movers
and they drank two quarts of whiskey.
They put African drums on the stereo
and went stamping around.

They pried the sanitation expert
off the side of the tank, and flushed him down
      the toilet.
They tore up the poster of Stevenson
and burned it in the fireplace.

Because the moving men wanted to
and he didn't have the heart to refuse.

The Hour of Feeling

Love, now a universal birth,
From heart to heart is stealing,
From earth to man, from man to earth:
—It is the hour of feeling.

—WORDSWORTH, "To My Sister"

A woman speaks:
"I hear you were in San Francisco.
What did they tell you about me?"

She begins to tremble. I can hear the sound
her elbow made, rapping on the wood.
It was something to see and to hear—
not like the words that pass for life,
things you read about in the papers.

People who read a deeper significance
into everything, every whisper . . .
who believe that a knife crossed with a fork
are a signal . . . by the sheer intensity
of their feeling leave an impression.

And with her, tangled in her hair,
came the atmosphere, four walls,
the avenues of the city
at twilight, the lights going on.

When I left I started to walk.
Once I stopped to look at a window
displaying ice skates and skis.
At another with Florsheim shoes . . .

Thanks to the emotion with which she spoke
I can see half of Manhattan,
the canyons and the avenues.

There are signs high in the air
above Times Square and the vicinity:
a sign for Schenley's Whiskey,
for Admiral Television,
and a sign saying Milltag, whatever that means.

I can see over to Brooklyn and Jersey,
and beyond there are meadows,
and mountains and plains.

The Rejected

I tried to explain why his manuscript had been
          rejected:
the writing was sincere, brilliant in places,
but our readers felt it would not appeal
to many people. It was too personal.

While I spoke he kept looking around.
A few feet away, the publicity woman
had stopped to talk to the office manager.
He seemed to think they were talking about him.

He told me that for years
X—naming a famous novelist—
had been entering his apartment
in his absence, and stealing his ideas.

I concluded by saying that I was sorry.
He took his glasses off and wiped them.
He shuffled the chapters, making them square.
Then, finally, he left.

I saw him again, months later
on Forty-second Street, looking up
at something he saw in a window,
or at the signs for tires and whiskey.

Since then I have envisioned him,
as Wordsworth says, wandering continually
from Twentieth Street up to Sixtieth,
and across from Eighth to Lexington Avenue.

The Sun and the Moon

"If the Sun and Moon should doubt,
They'd immediately go out."

When I try to think what they have in common
I have to say, paranoia.

An unshakable belief in their own importance . . .
They see what they desire.

Certainly, life would be a lot simpler.
You have to be mad, that's the catch.

As it is, I have no one to blame but myself.
I sit down to write . . .

An hour later the table is covered
        with words.
And then I start crossing them out.

The Mannequins

Whenever I passed Saks Fifth Avenue
I would stop at a certain window.
They didn't acknowledge my presence—they just stared.

He was sitting in his favorite chair,
smoking a pipe and reading a best seller.
She was standing in front of an easel.

She was finding it easy to paint
by filling in the numbered spaces
with colors. $5.98.

The artificial logs glowed in the fireplace.
Soon it would be Christmas. Santa would come down
        the chimney,
and they'd give each other presents.

She would give him skis and cuff links.
He would give her a watch with its works exposed,
and a fur coat, and perfume.

Though I knew it was "neurasthenic"
I couldn't help listening to the words
that they said without moving their lips.

Hubert's Museum

When I was young and used to wander
down to Times Square on a Saturday
to see a movie with social significance,
e.g., *The Battleship Potemkin,*

passing Hubert's Museum I'd look at pictures
of Ike and Mike, World Famous Midgets,
and Sahloo Snake Dancer,
and Princess Marie, the Ape with the Human Brain.

Now, looking back, it's not the crowd scene
on the steps that I remember—
"A marvel," *New Masses*, "of direction"—
nor the storming of the Winter Palace,

but the body of the Crocodile Man,
and the face of El Fusilado,
who "faced a firing squad, received 8 bullets
through the body and head, yet LIVED!"

Boots and Saddles

Mad Murray Kadish,
Nick D'Amato and Murray Chubinsky
were waiting on line outside the Paramount Theater

when an old guy came out of the alley
and said, "You fellers want to hear somethin?"
He was in the Seventh Cavalry.

You wouldn't believe it, he
had served in the U. S. Cavalry
in Mexico, under "Black Jack" Pershing.

At the time he was living with a Mex,
half-Indian girl.

Finally he was wise to her.
"Baby," he said, "you're a two-timer,
I'm wise to you and the lieutenant."

Now all he wanted was bus fare.
"What the hell," said Murray Chubinsky
and gave him fifty cents.

He looked at it, started walking,
then running down the alley,
and joined his friends in the Seventh Cavalry.

They sounded "Boots and Saddles"
and they all went riding off.

The Middleaged Man

There is a middleaged man, Tim Flanagan,
whom everyone calls "Fireball."
Every night he does the rocket-match trick.
"Ten, nine, eight . . ." On zero
p f f t! It flies through the air.

Walking to the subway with Flanagan . . .
He tells me that he lives out in Queens
on Avenue Street, the end of the line.
That he "makes his home" with his sister
who has recently lost her husband.

What is it to me?
Yet I can't help imagining what it would be like
to be Flanagan. Climbing the stairs
and letting himself in . . .
I can see him eating in the kitchen.

He stays up late watching television
From time to time he comes to the window.
At this late hour the streets are deserted.
He looks up and down. He looks right at me,
then he steps back out of sight.

*

Sometimes I wake in the middle of the night
and I have a vision of Flanagan.

He is wearing an old pair of glasses
with a wire bent around the ear
and fastened to the frame with tape.

He is reading a novel by Morley Callaghan.
Whenever I wake he is still there . . .
with his glasses. I wish he would get them fixed.
I cannot sleep as long as there is wire
running from his eye to his ear.

OK for Keats

"Keats said that truth is beauty—
I say just the opposite.
When I see truth in front of me
it has a terrible appearance."

Thus spake Mandelbaum,
sitting on the beach.
He was thin and somewhat sallow
from his work at the Hospital for Joint Diseases—
the hairs on his body glistening
like fish scales, flat and wet.

"Beauty was OK for Keats,
but ever since Buchenwald and Auschwitz
people have pictures in the back of their head—
emaciated human beings,
bodies stacked up like wood,
photographs of rooms full of shoes
and clothing arranged in piles.
Not to mention the atom bomb,
faces and bodies exposed to radiation.
That is truth. Where is the beauty?

I couldn't waste my time
reading English. When I raised an objection

they would tell me it was art
so it didn't have to make sense.

It's been a long time,"
he said, "but I seem to recall—
didn't Keats have medical training?
Didn't he work in a hospital?"

"He was a surgeon's apprentice."

"There you are. He ought to have known better."

Newspaper Nights

After midnight when the presses were rolling
we would leave the *Herald Tribune* building
and walk up to Times Square.
The three of us would still be laughing and joking.

I can see a sign that says Schenley.
There are numbers high on a building
telling the time, 12:27,
the temperature, 36.

We have the streets all to ourselves.
There is only the sound of an ambulance or a fire.
There are only the lights that still keep changing
from green to red and back to green in silence.

III

Searching for the Ox

Chimneys

These bare brown trunks and branches
are my destiny. Destiny fits
always—no doubt about it.
There can be no such thing as a life
that wasn't meant for the person who has it.

Every day I walk in the lane
to the cliff from where there's a view
of the harbor spread out, the town
and, on the far shore, the three chimneys
of the Long Island Lighting Company.

One way to live is to tell stories:
"Once upon a time there were three chimneys—
two with red and white rings around them.
The third was considerably shorter
and painted a plain brown."

Cliff Road

Walking on the road at night . . .
At regular intervals a street light
makes a green shelf in the leaves.
Houses give off a muffled sound—
TV, the murmur of voices
and roar of the studio audience.

From time to time a plane goes winking over,
heading for Kennedy or La Guardia.

You pass the house of Angelo Scalise
who came here from Chicago—
the biggest house on the street.
It seems there is always a limousine
parked near the gate, with a driver
who, when you pass, glances up.

Then the cottage back in the trees
inhabited by the Henderson sisters . . .
I have often seen them together
in the winter gathering sticks.

Then there is a slope and a path
that goes right down to the beach.
The fishers are sure to be there
surfcasting, in absolute silence,
side by side but at a distance.

They start casting at Connecticut
in the sunset at high tide
when the shore seems to be drifting.
Then it's dark, you no longer see them
but, as I said, they are there
you can tell, by a faint white splash.

The road itself continues,
narrowing. This is Lovers' Lane.
It ends at a fence on a cliff,
looking at the lights on the opposite shore.

Florida

A balloon drifting in a pool,
swivelling when the wind changes . . .

It tugs, trying to lift,
but is held by the wet string.

All through the afternoon it drifts
from one side of the pool to the other.

Baruch

I

There is an old folk saying:
"He wishes to study the Torah
but he has a wife and family."
Baruch had a sincere love of learning
but he owned a dress-hat factory.

One night he was in his cart returning
to the village. Falling asleep . . .
All at once he uttered a cry
and snatched up the reins. He flew!
In the distance there was fire
and smoke. It was the factory,
the factory that he owned was burning.

All night it burned, and by daylight
Lev Baruch was a ruined man.
Some said that it was gypsies,
that sparks from their fire set it burning.
Others said, the workers.

But Lev never murmured. To the contrary,
he said, "It is written,
'by night in a pillar of fire.' "
He said, "Every day of my life
I had looked for a sign in that direction.
Now that I have been relieved of my property
I shall give myself to the Word."

And he did from that day on,
reading Rashi and Maimonides.

He was half way over the *Four Mountains*
when one day, in the midst of his studying,
Lev Baruch fell sick and died.
For in Israel it is also written,
"Prophecy is too great a thing for Baruch."

II

They were lovers of reading in the family.
For instance, Cousin Deborah
who, they said, had read everything . . .
The question was, which would she marry,
Tolstoy or Lermontov or Pushkin?

But her family married her off
to a man from Kiev, a timber merchant
who came from Kiev with a team of horses.
On her wedding day she wept, .
and at night when they locked her in
she kicked and beat on the door.
She screamed. So much for the wedding!
As soon as it was daylight, Brodsky—
that was his name—drove back to Kiev
like a man pursued, with his horses.

III

We have been devoted to words.
Even here in this rich country
Scripture enters and sits down
and lives with us like a relative.
Taking the best chair in the house . . .

His eyes go everywhere, not missing anything.
Wherever his looks go, something ages

and suddenly tears or falls.
Here, a worn place in the carpet,
there, a crack in the wall.

The love of literature goes with us.

On a train approaching midnight
everyone else has climbed into his **sarcophagus**
except four men playing cards.
There is nothing better than poker—
not for the stakes but the companionship,
trying to outsmart one another.
Taking just one card . . .

I am sitting next to the window,
looking at the lights on the prairie
clicking by. From time to time
two or three will come together
then go wandering off again.

Then I see a face, pale and unearthly,
that is flitting along with the train,
passing over the fields and rooftops,
and I hear a voice out of the past:
"He wishes to study the Torah."

Mashkin Hill

When Levin mowed Mashkin Hill
there were moments of happy self-forgetfulness.
When he talked to a peasant who believed in God,
Levin realized that he too believed.

In the modern world there aren't any peasants.
They don't cut hay with a scythe,
or the women rake it in windrows.
Now all that work is done by machines.

Now the farmer comes home like anyone
to find that his wife has had her hair done,
and that they're dining by candlelight,
the children having been fed.

And there is no God for Levin
but the quietness of his house.

The Sanctuaries

"Come in. Don't bring the candle.
Here are the three dark sanctuaries:
the room of memorizing,
the room of reclining (the forge)
and the room of the critic.

The first you see are prophets
who converse with spirits and demons
that live in sea-mist and cloud—
genus irritabile vatum
weighted with the fate of the world.

These others stare at a wall
where thought appears, in images."
Then suddenly turning toward me,
she said, "Which kind are you?"
I said, "I stare at the wall."

"Tell me then, what do you see?"
"A dog running along a path
that leads down to the shore.
He disappears behind some bushes,
then reappears lower down."

"A dog," she said, "is that all?
Look again. What do you see now?"

"Two fishermen, wearing straw hats
that conceal their faces. They look Chinese.
The boat in which they sit seems to be drifting
on images—of the shore, with trees
and a white cloud standing over."

Searching for the Ox

1

I have a friend who works in a mental hospital.
Sometimes he talks of his patients.
There is one, a schizophrenic:
she was born during the Korean War
and raised on an Air Force base.
Then the family moved to La Jolla.
At fourteen she started taking speed
because everyone else was taking it.

Father, I too have my cases:
hands, eyes, voices, ephemera.
They want me to see how they live.
They single me out in a crowd, at a distance,
the one face that will listen
to any incoherent, aimless story.
Then for years they hang around—
"Hey listen!"—tugging at a nerve.
Like the spirits Buddhists call
"hungry ghosts." And when they sense an opening,
rush in. So they are born
and live. So they continue.

There is something in disorder that calls to me.
Out there beyond the harbor
where, every night, the lighthouse
probes the sea with its feathery beam,
something is rising to the surface.
It lies in the darkness breathing,

it floats on the waves regarding
this luminous world,
lights that are shining round the shoreline.
It snorts and splashes,
then rolls its blackness like a tube
back to the bottom.

At dusk when the lamps go on
I have stayed outside and watched
the shadow-life of the interior,
feeling myself apart from it.
A feeling of—as though I were made of glass.
Or the balloon I once saw in Florida
in a swimming pool, with a string
trailing in loops on the surface.
Suddenly the balloon went swivelling
on the water, trying to lift.
Then drifted steadily, being driven
from one side of the pool to the other.

2

There is a light in a window opposite.

All over the world . . . in China
and Africa, they are turning the pages.
All that is necessary is to submit
to engineering, law—one of the disciplines
that, when you submit, drive you forward.

There have been great strides in space.

On a flight leaving Kennedy
I have heard the engineers from IBM

speaking slide rule and doing their calculations.
I saw the first men leave for the moon:
how the rocket clawed at the ground
at first, reluctant to lift;
how it rose, and climbed, and curved,
punching a round, black hole in a cloud.
Before I got back to Orlando
it had been twice round the world.

And still, I must confess,
I fear those *messieurs*, like a peasant
listening to the priests talk Latin.
They will send me off to Heaven
when all I want is to live in the world.

3

The search for the ox continues.
I read in the *Times*, there are young men in Osaka
called Moles. They live underground
in the underground shopping center.
They cut a joint off their little finger,
and they say, "All Al Capone."

I have a friend who has left America—
he finds it more pleasant living in Italy.

O ruins, traditions!
Past a field full of stones,
the ruins of vine-wreathed brickwork,
the road in a soundless march continues
forever into the past.

I have sat in the field full of stones—
stones of an archway, stones

of the columns of the temple,
stones carved S.P.Q.R.,
stones that have been shaped
as women are . . .
Limbs of the gods that have fallen,
too cumbersome to be borne.

By the lake at Trasimeno . . .
If Hannibal had not paused at Trasimeno
the history of the world would have been different.
How so? There would still be a sound
of lapping water, and leaves.

4

"As you have wasted your life here in this corner
you have ruined it all over the world."
This was written by Cavafy who lived in Alexandria.
Alexandria, with blue awnings
that flap in the wind,
sea-walls gleaming with reflections.
A steam-winch rattles,
an anchor clanks,
smoke drifts over the rooftops,
and at night the lighted streets go sailing.

At night the gods come down—
the earth then seems so pleasant.
They pass through the murmuring crowd.
They are seen in the cafés and restaurants.
They prefer the voice of a child
or the face of a girl to their fame
in their high, cold palaces on Olympus.

In the evening the wind blows from the sea.
The wind rises and winds like a serpent

filling the diaphanous curtains
where the women sit: Mousmé,
Hélène, and the English girl.
When you pass, their lips make a sound,
twittering, like the swallows
in Cyprus that built their nests
in the temple, above the door.
Each one has a sweetheart far away.
They are making their trousseaux;
they don't make love, they knit.

In the bar down the street
a door keeps opening and closing.
Then a pair of heels go hurrying.
In the streets that lead down to the harbor
all night long there are footsteps
and opening doors. It is Eros
Peridromos, who never sleeps till dawn.

5

Following in the Way
that "regards sensory experience as relatively
          unimportant,"
and that aims to teach the follower
"to renounce what one is attached to"—
in spite of this dubious gift
that would end by negating poetry altogether,
in the practice of meditating
on the breath, I find my awareness
of the world—the cry of a bird,
susurrus of tires, the wheezing

of the man in the chair next to me—
has increased. That every sound
falls like a pebble into a well,
sending out ripples that seem to be continuing
through the universe. Sound has a tail
that whips around the corner;
I try not to follow. In any case,
I find I am far more aware
of the present, sensory life.

I seem to understand what the artist
was driving at; every leaf stands clear
and separate. The twig seems to quiver
with intellect. Searching for the ox
I come upon a single hoofprint.
I find the ox, and tame it,
and lead it home. In the next scene
the moon has risen, a cool light.
Both the ox and herdsman vanished.

There is only earth:
in winter laden with snow,
in summer covered with leaves.

IV

Further Adventures of the Letter I

Happiness

Passing meadows and farmland . . .
I turn off the road into a lane
that is shadowed by ancient trees.

I know that everyone will be there.
My aunts, none of whom ever married
but who, thank God, are "as well as could be
      expected" . . .

Father greets me, hiding his affection
as usual. And Peter . . . he can't wait
to grow up like me and be a soldier.

Grandmother enters, leaning on Grandfather's arm.
He is still erect, with the look
that "seems to go right through one."

          *

Next day I accompany my father
on a tour of the fields. It is the harvest.
The mowers are out . . . bare legs and yellow
      hair.

He complains . . . they can't be trusted
with machinery. They left out the harrow
in the night dew, and now it is covered with rust.

          *

In the door of a cottage as I pass
a woman wearing a red kerchief
is singing and playing the balalaika.

I travel on, skirting the forest where wolves are
            reported,
and a she-bear. Rising on her hind legs
she is higher than two men and as wide as a door.

The road winds on past field and farmland.
The poplars that follow the stream are rippling
and sounds at a distance are borne by the wind.

The Tree Seat

They are sitting outdoors
on the deck, and the sound carries—
a voice that says "cope"
and a voice that says "meaningful."

The house, the first time I saw it,
was cluttered with brown furniture.
The old man, Anderson, the owner,
sat, in the turtleneck sweater
he always had on, with soupspots,
clasping the head of a walking stick.
His hands were terribly swollen;
he could hardly walk, for arthritis.
But he kept everything in repair;
he fixed the plumbing, even the wiring.

What did I think of this Kennedy fellow?
He was a Navy man himself.
He had a photograph somewhere . . .
He pushed with his arms and stood
and crossed the room with his walking stick.

                    *

One day he built a tree seat.
This takes a bit of explaining.
The land on our side of the street
slopes down, and the trees reach up
and fork just at street level.

One day the old man came with a board
and a hammer. He nailed the board
in the fork of a tree. Then sat.
When I looked up, there he'd be.
There was a poet, Mayakovsky,
who wrote of a "cloud of trousers"—
he should have seen the cloud formation
surging in the boughs above me.

I'd be hurrying out to the car
when the old man would waylay me
to talk about . . . lake fishing.
Thirty or forty years ago
he would get up very early,
tie his tackle to the running board
and drive to a mountain lake.
When he arrived, at daybreak,
he would keep an eye out for dragonflies—
he used dragonfly larva for bait.

He would fill the can with larva,
then row from shore, ship oars,
throw out a line, and drift.

*

This couldn't go on.
Living by himself like this was too dangerous.
Someone wrote to the old man's daughter
and she came and took him away.

The next we heard, he was in Florida.
Then he died, and the house was sold.
They hired interior decorators—
who knocked out walls, made a picture window,
and a deck with a view of the bay.

In summer every sound carries.
I can't help hearing the conversation . . .
Charlie's voice—he's a celebrity
in his field, public relations;

a positive voice—that's Eleanor;

and the wind moving in the boughs
with a creaking sound, like oarlocks
on the water a long way off.

A Donkey Named Hannibal

At times I am visited by a donkey
who was once the great soldier Hannibal.

The reason he didn't take Rome,
he says, was a fear of success.

Now that he has been psychoanalyzed
he would, he is confident, rise to the occasion.

But then he wouldn't be Hannibal.
People would say, "It's a donkey."

So, once more, Hannibal has decided . . .
Moreover, if he succeeded it wouldn't be Rome.

The Street

Here comes the subway grating fisher
letting down his line through the sidewalk.

Yesterday there was the running man
who sobbed and wept as he ran.

Today there is the subway grating fisher.
Standing as if in thought . . .

He fishes a while. Then winds up the line
and continues to walk, looking down.

The Judgement of Paris

All day the trumpet sounded and they came
marching toward the memorial.

The Indianapolis war memorial.
It is covered with flags and cannonballs.

It looks as though when the surface was still wet
they threw things at it, and by God they stuck.

*

There were three jolly visiting firemen,
one of them carrying a cattle prod.

Leaning on it. A secretary passed
and *wham!* he gave her a shock.

*

Then there were the three middleaged women
at the Sheridan, going up.

They had all had their hair set.
Suddenly one who wore glasses turned to me

and held out . . . a roll of toilet paper.
"Here," she said, "wanna have a crap game?"

Then they all three started giggling,
and then they all got off.

The Daled

Across the room the night city editor
has turned his face toward me
with a curious, mild stare.
Waiting for copy . . .

Later in the evening there will be a crowd
at Jack's. Discussing sports . . .
Some old codger holding forth—
what His Honor said to the Commissioner.
And there will be the usual four.

According to an ancient fable
there are thirty-six "hidden saints."
It could be the tailor, the shoemaker,
it could be a Regular Army colonel—
as long as there are thirty-six
the world will not come to an end.

Also there are the Daled—four newspapermen
who are always playing poker.
As long as this situation continues
God will hold back the final catastrophe.
"What's that? It sounds like water."
"Wait a minute," says Shapiro.
"We're here to play cards. Whose deal is it?"

"I'll see your five," says Flanagan,
"and raise it."

So the game goes on
from week to week. I have known them to begin
late at night when everything is silent
and to play right through till dawn.

Tsushima

Under the administrations of Presidents Johnson
        and Nixon
everyone was at sea, like the Russians
in the days of the last Tsars:
all the middle-class houses steaming
full speed ahead in a fog.

The buildings of concrete and glass,
streets lined with telephone poles,
were like the fleet leaving for Tsushima,
sailing around the world, to explode
and sink in hideous steam.

I was living at the time in California.
Every night when the sea-mist rose
gliding over the trees and rooftops,
I heard it whispering, "Tsushima."

Big Dream, Little Dream

The Elgonyi say, there are big dreams and little dreams.
The little dream is just personal . . .
Sitting in a plane that is flying
too close to the ground. There are wires . . .
on either side there's a wall.

The big dream feels significant.
The big dream is the kind the president has.
He wakes and tells it to the secretary,
together they tell it to the cabinet,
and before you know there is war.

Before the Poetry Reading

Composition for Voices, Dutch Banjo, Sick Flute,
and a Hair Drum

I

This is the poetry reading.
This is the man who is going to give the poetry reading.
He is standing in a street in which the rain is falling
With his suitcase open on the roof of a car for some reason,
And the rain falling into the suitcase,
While the people standing nearby say,
"If you had come on a Monday,
Or a Tuesday, or a Thursday,
If you had come on a Wednesday,
Or on any day but this,
You would have had an audience,
For we here at Quinippiac (Western, or Wretched State U.)
Have wonderful audiences for poetry readings."
By this time he has closed the suitcase
And put it on the back seat, which is empty,
But on the front seat sit Saul Bellow,
James Baldwin, and Uncle Rudy and Fanya.
They are upright, not turning their heads, their fedoras
       straight on,
For they know where they are going,
And you should know, so they do not deign to answer
When you say, "Where in Hell is this car going?"
Whereupon, with a leap, slamming the door shut,
Taking your suitcase with it, and your Only Available
       Manuscript,
And leaving you standing there,
The car leaps into the future,

Still raining, in which its taillight disappears.
And a man who is still looking on
With his coat collar turned up, says
"If you had come on a Friday,
A Saturday or a Sunday,
Or if you had come on a Wednesday
Or a Tuesday, there would have been an audience.
For we here at Madagascar
And the University of Lost Causes
Have wonderful audiences for poetry readings."

II

This is the man who is going to introduce you.
He says, "Could you tell me the names
Of the books you have written.
And is there anything you would like me to say?"

III

This is the lady who is giving a party for you
After the poetry reading.
She says, "I hope you don't mind, but
I have carefully avoided inviting
Any beautiful, attractive farouche young women,
But the Vicar of Dunstable is coming,
Who is over here this year on an exchange program,
And the Calvinist Spiritual Chorus Society,
And all the members of the Poetry Writing Workshop."

IV

This is the man who has an announcement to make.
He says, "I have a few announcements.
First, before the poetry reading starts,

If you leave the building and walk rapidly
Ten miles in the opposite direction,
A concert of music and poetry is being given
By Wolfgang Amadeus Mozart and William Shakespeare.
Also, during the intermission
There is time for you to catch the rising
Of the Latter Day Saints at the Day of Judgement.
Directly after the reading,
If you turn left, past the Community Building,
And walk for seventeen miles,
There is tea and little pieces of eraser
Being served in the Gymnasium.
Last week we had a reading by Dante,
And the week before by Sophocles;
A week from tonight, Saint Francis of Assisi
         will appear in person—
But tonight I am happy to introduce
Mister Willoughby, who will make the introduction
Of our guest, Mr. Jones."

                    V

This has been the poetry reading.

The Shelling Machine

I have found a new heaven
and earth-the food tastes different.
I am rearranging my senses.
The Fates, who are members of my family
with definite ideas about everyone,
what would they think, seeing me in a village
on a mountain in Macedonia?

My ancestors came from a house like this
with a window that is painted on.
Many years ago they went to America.
That was to be their life and mine.
Yet here I am, eating *kievski šašlik*
and looking at a wedding party
as it climbs up the side of the mountain.

A bride dressed in white
led by three musicians . . .
I have changed my psyche by coming here
to this remote, unheard-of place.

*

At the side of the road stands a box
like a sedan chair, with four handles.
On closer inspection a machine . . .
Inside are a number of cogs
worked by a crank, like a mangle.
Then a carrier and a spout . . .
I have it—a shelling machine!

Not one but seven, just painted—
so this is the local factory.

They manufacture these box-mangles
and ship them out of the village
in the consciousness of a total stranger
overseas, with their fresh blue paint
and sticky yellow handles.

There'll be a day when the contraption
has been standing at the edge of a field
till all the colors have faded
and the cogs are trying to come loose.
Yet it will still be grinding out music
in the memory of a total stranger,
like a squeeze-box.

In turn, I have changed the machine.
No one else would have stopped to look at it—
certainly none of the people
who work there every day in the field.

The Driving Instructor

I overtook a man who was walking with the aid of two metal canes with arm-grips. He spoke to me explaining that he had a weak heart and asking me to assist him. I did, walking beside him and letting him hold on to my arm as we crossed the street. Then I stayed with him for several blocks.

He was born in France, of Yugoslav parents. He had been to Yugoslavia as a journalist. He was now working in a driving school. I said this must be dangerous. He said no, for there were double controls, so he didn't worry.

I said that life in France was dear. He said it cost 30,000 francs for a meal in one of the restaurants we were passing, 50,000 in another. Old francs, he said, for I must have looked astonished. He said that foreigners came to France and they were hit ("*on les tape*"). People seemed to think all foreigners were rich—this wasn't so, many of them had made economies in order to come. What did they want? To drink a little. But the minute "they" saw a pigeon they hit him.

I said that bad things could happen to foreigners in any country, and then they would think all the people were bad, but this wasn't so. My son Tony's suitcase had been ransacked at one of the airports, his Super 8 millimeter movies stolen. Tony had asked, "Why did the man do that to me?" and I had told him that some people did these things, but he must not therefore think badly of all people.

The driving instructor listened to this without saying a word. I expected him to say that he understood my feelings on the subject and approved of the way I had handled it, but he only listened with a faint smile.

We parted at the Boulevard St. Michel, shaking hands. He said that his car was across the street. It had been a pleasure. I said, for me too—it had been pleasure.